Envenomators

DEADLY FROGS!

by Meish Goldish

Consultant: Professor Bryan Grieg Fry
Head of Venom Evolution Laboratory
School of Biological Sciences
University of Queensland, Australia

BEARPORT
PUBLISHING

New York, New York

Credits

Cover, © Renato Augusto Martins/CC BY-SA/4.0; TOC, © Carlos Jared; 4T, © Carlos Jared; 4B, © AGB Photo Library Produções Fotográficas Ltda; 5TL, © Ondrej Prosicky/Shutterstock; 5TR, © JasonOndreicka/iStock; 5BL, © WildPhotos/Dreamstime; 5BR, © Vince Adam/Shutterstock; 6T, © Carlos Jared; 6B, © Carlos Jared; 8L, © Mark Moffett/Minden Pictures; 8R, © Carlos Jared; 9, © Carlos Jared; 10T, © Nutjarin Moolnamai/Dreamstime; 10B, © nkbimages/iStock; 11, © Leonardo/Fotolia; 12T, © Dirk Ercken/Dreamstime; 12BL, © Dirk Ercken/Dreamstime; 12BR, © reptiles4all/iStock; 13, © Filipe Frazao/Shutterstock; 14, © JialiangGao/GFDL; 15T, © Dirk Ercken/Shutterstock; 15B, © Kleinermann82/Dreamstime; 16, © Carlos Jared; 17, © Photowitch/Dreamstime; 18, © Mauro Teixeira Jr; 19, © Dirk Ercken/Shutterstock; 20T, © Claudio Contreras/NPL/Minden Pictures; 20B, © Webguzs/iStock; 21, © FLPA/Alamy; 22 (L to R), © Ricardo Marques, © Pedro Peloso, and © Dirk Ercken/Dreamstime; 24, © Dirk Ercken/Shutterstock.

Publisher: Kenn Goin
Creative Director: Spencer Brinker
Photo Researcher: Thomas Persano

Library of Congress Cataloging-in-Publication Data

Names: Goldish, Meish, author.
Title: Deadly frogs / by Meish Goldish.
Description: New York, New York : Bearport Publishing, [2019] | Series:
  Envenomators | Includes bibliographical references
  and index.
Identifiers: LCCN 2018010870 (print) | LCCN 2018012092 (ebook) |
  ISBN 9781684027040 (ebook) | ISBN 9781684026586 (library)
Subjects: LCSH: Dendrobatidae—Juvenile literature.
Classification: LCC QL668.E233 (ebook) | LCC QL668.E233 G65 2019 (print) |
  DDC 597.8/77—dc23
LC record available at https://lccn.loc.gov/2018010870

For more information, write to Bearport Publishing Company, Inc., 45 West 21st Street, Suite 3B, New York, New York 10010. Printed in the United States of America.

10 9 8 7 6 5 4 3 2 1

Contents

Terrible Pain

In 2015, a scientist named Carlos Jared was collecting frogs in a **scrubland** in Brazil. One day, he spotted a small, brown frog and grabbed it with his bare hands. Almost instantly, Carlos felt a sharp pain shooting up and down his arm. He was puzzled—what was causing the terrible discomfort?

Brazilian scientist Carlos Jared

Carlos Jared was collecting frogs in an area of Brazil called Caatinga—a dry, desertlike place with small trees and bushes.

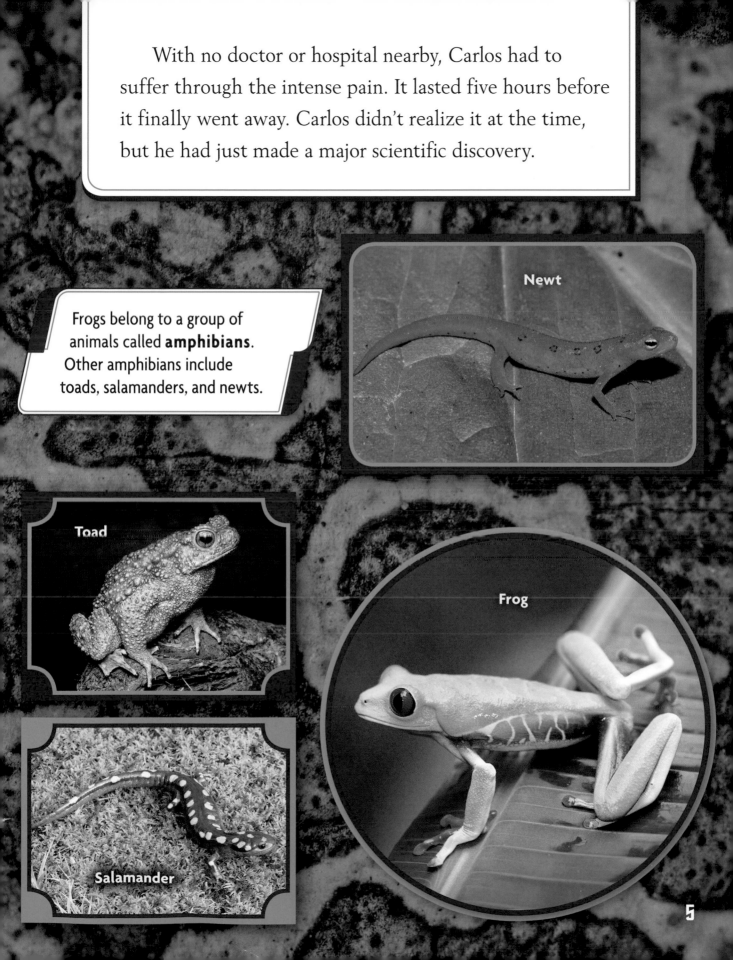

With no doctor or hospital nearby, Carlos had to suffer through the intense pain. It lasted five hours before it finally went away. Carlos didn't realize it at the time, but he had just made a major scientific discovery.

Frogs belong to a group of animals called **amphibians**. Other amphibians include toads, salamanders, and newts.

Newt

Toad

Frog

Salamander

Mystery Solved

Later, in a **laboratory**, Carlos examined the creature, which he discovered was a Greening's frog. He then understood what had happened to his hand. "It took me a long time to realize that my pain was related to my careless collection of the frog," he said. Using a **microscope**, Carlos was amazed to see tiny needlelike spines covering the frog's head and upper lip—almost like a spiky helmet.

A Greening's frog is about 3 inches (8 cm) long.

Carlos Jared at work in a laboratory

When Carlos picked up the frog, it pushed its spines into his hand. The spines broke his skin and **injected venom** into his body. Until then, scientists didn't know of any frogs that produced venom and could inject it. Through his painful accident, Carlos had discovered the first kind of venomous frog!

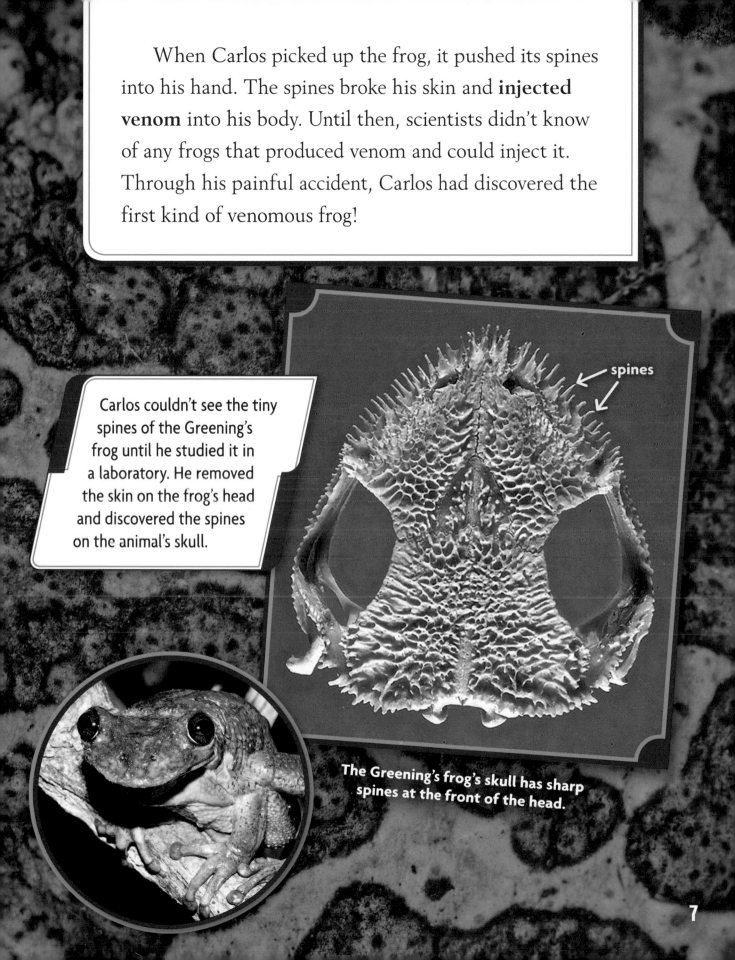

Carlos couldn't see the tiny spines of the Greening's frog until he studied it in a laboratory. He removed the skin on the frog's head and discovered the spines on the animal's skull.

spines

The Greening's frog's skull has sharp spines at the front of the head.

A Second Discovery

Soon after Carlos's **encounter**, scientists in a Brazilian rain forest made a second amazing find. They discovered another venomous frog—the Bruno's casque-headed frog. Like the Greening's frog, the Bruno's frog has spines on its head that inject venom into attackers.

The venom of a Bruno's casque-headed frog is 25 times more powerful than the venom of a deadly Brazilian pit viper snake.

Bruno's casque-headed frog

Brazilian pit viper snake

A Bruno's frog is about 12 times deadlier than a Greening's frog. A single gram (0.035 oz) of a Bruno's venom is strong enough to kill 80 people—or 300,000 mice. American scientist Edmund Brodie, Jr., said, "We were amazed at the level of **toxins** in these frogs." However, one Bruno's frog produces only a tiny amount of venom, which rarely causes death.

Greening's frogs and Bruno's casque-headed frogs were first discovered in the 1800s. However, scientists didn't realize that these frogs could inject venom until 2015.

A Bruno's casque-headed frog is about the same size as a Greening's frog.

Frog Studies

After discovering both kinds of venomous frogs, scientists were eager to learn more about them. They studied 15 Greening's frogs and 15 Bruno's casque-headed frogs. They **analyzed** the gooey white venom that the frogs produced. The scientists wondered: *Where does the venom come from?*

A scientist uses a microscope to study a specimen.

Scientists cut open dead frogs in order to learn more about their bodies.

Scientists found **glands** that make venom inside the frog's skin. These glands supply venom to the spines in the frog's head. When a **predator** attacks, the frog bobs its head up and down or side to side to jab the enemy with its spines. The venom then gets injected into the predator's **bloodstream**.

A Bruno's casque-headed frog rests on a tree.

Scientists discovered that the sharp spines of venomous frogs help keep enemies from eating them. Carlos Jared says, "Swallowing one of these frogs might be similar to trying to swallow a cactus."

11

Other Deadly Frogs

Greening's and Bruno's casque-headed frogs are the only frogs known to inject venom into their attackers. However, they're not the only kinds of deadly frogs. Some frogs are dangerous because their bodies produce poison that coats their skin. If a predator touches a poisonous frog, it can get sick and die.

Poisonous frogs are usually brightly colored. For example, they may have combinations of red, blue, yellow, and other hues.

One drop of poison from certain frogs is so strong that it can kill up to 20 people! If an animal eats the frog and lives, the poison can make it very sick. The toxins can **irritate** an attacker's eyes or mouth—and it can even **paralyze** a human.

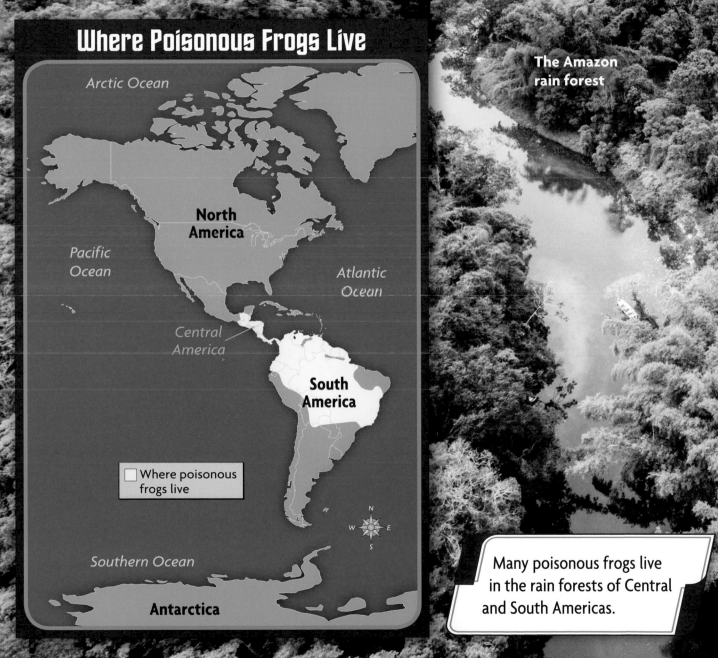

Where Poisonous Frogs Live

Arctic Ocean

North America

Pacific Ocean

Atlantic Ocean

Central America

South America

☐ Where poisonous frogs live

Southern Ocean

Antarctica

The Amazon rain forest

Many poisonous frogs live in the rain forests of Central and South Americas.

Powerful Poison

The deadliest kind of poisonous frogs are poison dart frogs. They get their name from native people in South America, who use the frogs' poison on **blow darts** when they hunt. To collect the poison, the hunters press the darts into the frog's skin, until poison covers the weapons. Then the hunters shoot the poisonous darts at animals they want to catch. A single drop of poison can kill a bird or small **mammal**.

A hunter uses a long tube to shoot a blow dart.

Poison dart frogs are deadly and tiny. Most grow just 1 to 2 inches (2.5 to 5 cm) long—that's about as small as a bottle cap! Yet each tiny frog has enough poison to coat up to 50 darts. Once the poison is applied to the dart, it remains **potent** for up to one year.

The golden poison frog is considered one of the most toxic animals in the world.

Poison dart frogs live in trees or under leaves, rocks, and logs on the rain forest floor. The frogs use their sticky tongues to catch ants, spiders, and flies.

Poison dart frogs are some of the smallest frogs in the world.

Venomous or Poisonous?

Scientists now know about two types of deadly frogs: venomous and poisonous. The Greening's and the Bruno's casque-headed frogs are venomous. About 220 other kinds of frogs are poisonous. Since all these frogs are deadly, what, exactly, is the difference between them? It's the way in which the frogs use their deadly weapons.

ENVENOMATORS:
The Bruno's casque-headed frog (on the left) and the Greening's frog (on the right) jab attackers with their sharp, venom-filled spines.

Venomous frogs use their needle-sharp spines to inject venom into attackers. Poisonous frogs do not inject anything. Instead, they **secrete** poison onto their own body. Then, if a predator touches the frog, the attacker can get sick and die.

POISONERS:
Poison dart frogs produce poison on their skin that can sicken or kill attackers.

Scientists believe that poisonous frogs get their poison from the insects they eat. If they are not fed poisonous insects, the frogs no longer produce poison.

Frog Defenses

Deadly frogs use their toxins to fight enemies. However, these frogs have other ways to protect themselves. Some venomous frogs use **camouflage** to hide from predators. Greening's frogs crawl inside small holes in trees, for example. A frog might plug up the tree hole with its head. Then enemies have a hard time seeing it, since the Greening's dark head blends in with the tree bark.

The brownish-green color of a Greening's frog makes the animal hard to spot on or in a tree.

If a predator finds a Greening's frog in a tree, it still might not attack because of the frog's venomous spines.

Poisonous frogs use bad-tasting poison and bright colors to stay safe. After a predator tastes a poison frog, it remembers the frog's colors and foul flavor. Then, it won't attack another frog with the same colors. The bright colors serve as a kind of "poison alert" for predators.

The bright colors of poison dart frogs tell other animals "stay away!"

Research Today

Today, scientists are still learning more about venomous and poisonous frogs. For example, researchers are now studying the toxins secreted by poison dart frogs. They hope one day these toxins can be used to create new medicines that will relax a person's muscles, **stimulate** the heart, or reduce pain.

A researcher gathers poison from a frog.

In the rain forests of Peru, some native people apply the poison of giant tree frogs to their skin. They believe the substance can cure **depression**, heart problems, and stomach pain. Scientists are investigating whether their claims are true.

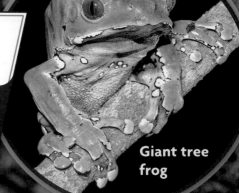

Giant tree frog

Scientists also believe that Greening's and Bruno's casque-headed frogs may not be the only kinds of venomous frogs. American scientist Dr. Deborah Hutchinson said, "There are likely more **species** of venomous frogs awaiting discovery." The possibility of discovering new species of deadly frogs has scientists very excited. Bryan Fry, a venomous animals researcher, said, "This is very, very cool."

A scientist collecting a tree frog on a bamboo plant

Deadly Frogs
— PROFILES —

	Bruno's Casque-Headed Frog (An Envenomator)	Greening's Frog (An Envenomator)	Poison Dart Frog (A Poisoner)

DESCRIPTION	A Bruno's casque-headed frog is a small, brown, spotted frog, with glands that produce deadly venom. Its head is covered in sharp, needlelike spines.	A Greening's frog is a small, brownish-green frog that lives in Brazil. Its head is covered with sharp, needle-like spines. The frog uses its spines to inject venom into attackers.	Native to South America, a poison dart frog is a tiny, brightly colored frog that secretes poison onto its skin. It is one of the most toxic frogs in the world.
LENGTH	About 3 inches (8 cm)	About 3 inches (8 cm)	1 to 2 inches (2.5 to 5 cm)
VENOM/POISON and Its Effects	The venom causes severe pain. One gram (0.035 oz) of Bruno's casque-headed frog venom, which is much more than a single frog produces, can kill about 80 people or 300,000 mice.	The venom causes severe pain. One gram (0.035 oz) of Greening's frog venom, which is much more than a single frog produces, can kill about 7 people, or 25,000 mice.	A poison dart frog's poison is strong enough to kill 20 people.

Glossary

amphibians (am-FIB-ee-uhnz) animals that have a backbone and live part of their lives in water and part on land

analyzed (AN-uh-lized) studied carefully

bloodstream (BLUHD-streem) blood circulating through the body

blow darts (BLOH DARTS) small pointed objects shot by blowing them through a long, narrow tube

camouflage (KAM-uh-flahzh) coloring that makes an animal look like its surroundings

depression (di-PRESH-uhn) a mood disorder marked by great sadness and hopelessness

encounter (en-KOUN-tur) an unexpected meeting, often unpleasant

glands (GLANDZ) body parts that produce chemicals

injected (in-JEKT-id) used a needle or needlelike instrument to put liquid into a body

irritate (IHR-uh-tate) to annoy or bother

laboratory (LAB-ruh-tor-ee) a place used by scientists to conduct experiments

mammal (MAM-uhl) a warm-blooded animal that has hair and drinks its mother's milk as a baby

microscope (MYE-kruh-skope) a tool used to see things that are too small to be seen with the eyes alone

paralyze (PA-ruh-lize) to cause something to be unable to move

potent (POH-tuhnt) powerful or strong

predator (PRED-uh-tur) an animal that hunts other animals for food

scrubland (SKRUB-land) a dry area with short trees and low bushes

secrete (sih-KREET) to produce a liquid from a gland and then discharge it

species (SPEE-sheez) types of animals or plants

stimulate (STIM-yuh-late) to start or increase activity in the body

toxins (TOKS-inz) poisonous substances

venom (VEN-uhm) toxic substances made by some animals

Index

Bibliography

Halliday, Tim. *The Book of Frogs: A Life-Size Guide to Six Hundred Species from Around the World.* Chicago: The University of Chicago (2015).

Turner, Pamela. *The Frog Scientist (Scientists in the Field Series).* Boston: Houghton Mifflin Harcourt (2011).

Read More

Bredeson, Carmen. *Poison Dart Frogs Up Close.* New York: Enslow Elementary (2012).

Dussling, Jennifer. *Deadly Poison Dart Frogs (Gross-Out Defenses).* New York: Bearport (2009).

Learn More Online

To learn more about venomous and poisonous frogs, visit
www.bearportpublishing.com/Envenomators

About the Author

Meish Goldish has written more than 300 books for children.
He lives in Brooklyn, New York.